Vertical Slicing and Boost Value Delivery

Slicing user stories in Agile software development

TJ Rerob

Contents

CONTENTS

Chapter One

Agile software development is a fluid environment

Agile software development is a complex environment. This work can be extremely difficult to understand and execute on in the timeframes required. At a high level, this is because the job to be done is unknown. Or in other words, how to accomplish the goals of the work, is unknown.

When starting on work, an Agile team is often simultaneously seeking to understand goals of the work while also creating a game plan to meet said goals. I would say it is more often than not, that teams don't know exactly how to accomplish the work when they first start. They must work on the problem and create the solution as they go.

Agile software development is also an environment that is full of change, where goals evolve and shift. Requiring the work to change to meet the goals. The work goals and how to meet the goals become even more difficult when mixed into this fluid environment.

All of this causes a lot of stress and pressure for the team. Let's get into some reasons for that further. As the benefits of Vertical Slicing become all the more clear when you fully understand the problems facing the team.

Software development causes pressure

Working against deadlines in software is normal and causes great pressure. Teams have to balance the work with due dates. Agile teams often have due dates created for work before they even start the work. Or dates created before the work is fully understood.

Lastly still, until work is far enough along and near completion, there are still unknowns. So until that point is reached, it can be impossible to say when work would be done. Yet all scenarios occur and have due dates created, without the work really driving when that date can be accomplished.

I would make 1 side point on due dates here. There are often due dates in business that are real and justified. They require certain work to be done before that date. I argue that we transfer the work of understanding due dates and make it about when the work can be completed. When the real question should be when do we need to start the work, to enable completion in time. This is also helped by the concept to be addressed.

So, how do you approach Agile software work in an environment like this? How do you write user stories to mitigate the issue of being up against deadlines? What practice will help you to write better user stories?

The answer is Vertical Slicing. This will help you avoid rushing work and quality. It allows incremental and iterative delivery of user stories. Building to larger goals. Ultimately though, it will boost your Delivery!

Problems encountered that add to the stress

Problems encountered in Agile software development that add to this stress. Let's recap them here in a nice list.

- Deadlines set arbitrarily, IE, without knowing the work
- Deadlines are too short
- The work is not understood
- Goals are not understood
- Work is in too big of chunks to get continuous feedback and incremental updates
- Not enough time to test
- Working on things that don't provide value
- Too long between getting value
- Deadlines set by those not involved with the details of the work
- Work done without real user interaction and understanding of what gains value
- Work is too complex in order to enable starting the work

That is a nice list of issues. I'm sure it is not all the issues, but it certainly covers a lot of what Agile software development teams run into.

Can you lump these all into a single issue?

How do you condense that to a single problem? To me, its all about the big bang mindset. Where you must address everything at once.

Above all, the pressure comes from the idea that you have to deliver everything at once.

There are lots of reasons for the stress, and exploring them is not the intent here. Instead, focusing on what can be done to help deliver user stories more effectively. This is doing work in pieces with Vertical Slicing. Doing in pieces is part of an incremental and iterative approach. Which is a driving force in Vertical Slices and Agile. Vertical Slices go a step further, in that they are pieces that work on their own.

So knowing all of this, what practices are out there to help?

You must consider a practice or a process where you work by understanding pieces of a system. Also understanding how those pieces work together in manageable chunks of work. Work that can be executed on in smaller timeframes.

Doing this way goes a long ways to enabling efficient Agile software development. It enables you to build the right things. It also helps avoid issues and rework. There is one last thing it gets you too. A nice cherry on top of all of these other benefits.

That cherry on top is Value! Working in such a way helps enable consistent and strong value in the work being done. So what process helps with all of this? It is Vertical Slicing of your user stories.

We will get into this more, just remember those ideas. Vertical Slices will boost your delivery and speed. Reduce complexity, and speed up time to done.

The cherry on top

So about this cherry on top of all the benefits of Vertical Slicing. Let's continue to explore it. For Agile teams working in to use Vertical Slicing of their user stories, the cherry is the consistent delivery of functionality and value.

Agile development using vertically sliced user stories enables the work to be done by the team and avoids the pressure associated with software development.

Bullet list of the eBook

In the following, I discuss Vertical Slicing. We will explore what the concept is. You will see it presented via how it makes up the components of a system. Using those components, we will explore how you liken things together to help drive out the work to be done. After this we will further explore the benefits of using this practice and some questions to help drive and organize your user stories.

Here is an outline of the ideas shown. So, experience the benefits today, and boost your delivery!

- What is Vertical Slicing
- Visual of the layers
- Consider the like things
- Benefits of using this
- Time to delivery in Agile and Waterfall
- It gains business value in the iteration
- 5 Best Questions to help break apart user stories into Vertical Slices

Let's get going!

Chapter Two

What is Vertical Slicing?

Vertical Slicing is where you slim down a work item to a narrow focus. In other words, breaking the work into small pieces. Yet, the pieces have all the functions to be stand-alone. It may or may not require more features to truly be useful. However, as a piece of the system, it works on its own.

Work items have just enough scope and functionality, plus just enough coverage across all system components involved, to be fully functional. It's as much art as it is science, in determining what is not enough, enough, or too much to be included in scope and functionality. That is often a factor of the team's typical output.

The key thing to remember is that you want all pieces of the system components to be included, so that the work can function with this piece of work.

Ultimately, this is a process of breaking up work. A way to split up larger features and functionality into more bite sized pieces of work. Work that an Agile software development team can go execute on. Also, work that once executed on, it could be completed and gain some value.

Practicing this will allow the agile team to improve in agile. It is really key to writing better user stories. More importantly, user stories that are likely to be completed and delivered.

An example

Let's start with an example of Vertical Slicing of user stories. Take a field on a website. Just a single field. That field only could be a Vertical Slice of work. The field includes the front end. It also has the database to store the value. Lastly, the service to store and update data to the website. Altogether, that work is limited in scope to just the single field. Yet, altogether, those pieces are complete and that field could function on its own.

Another definition to consider

Another way to describe Vertical Slicing is to say that the piece of work goes across all system layers. They can include, but not limited to, the user interface, database, and services or logic used.

Chapter Three

Vertical Slice of the System Layers

To help show the Vertical Slicing Agile idea, consider this. First, breaking down features of work into small pieces. Second, if small enough, group like pieces. The groupings I call "like things". An example is similar fields or actions on a website. Group the fields together, as they behave and function similarly. These help to show the Vertical Slicing Agile concept.

Piece of Each Layer

The visual below shows a Vertical Slice. These are common areas of a system. The user interface, services, and database. Vertical Slicing takes a piece of each layer. Together, the pieces make up a slice of work.

This is to say a small piece of the user interface or front end. In addition, a small piece of the service used. Lastly, a small piece of the database. Together, those small pieces are a Vertical Slice of work. Together, they deliver a piece of work, without being the entirety of any of the separate layers.

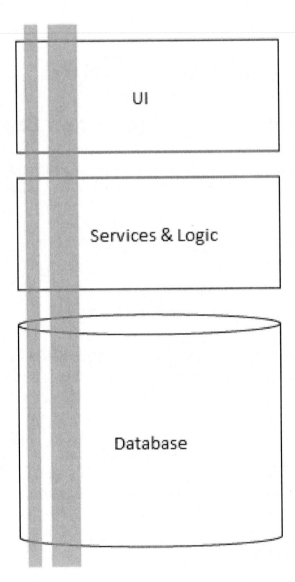

Agile Time to Delivery

Vertical Slicing the work across the system layers are key to consistent delivery in Agile Software Development

Next is What I Call "Like Things"

Next, is the idea of "like things". This is where you group similar items. So that you could work them together. However, only if they are similar and could be completed in a sprint. When they relate enough and are small enough, they can be a Vertical Slice of work. This is the "like things" idea to me.

Think of an average website. If you break up pieces of the site into like things, those could be Vertical Slices. Or pieces of them could be. Group together similar pieces of the site. Those are your "like things". IE, the menu, or navigation. Taking one of those individually, you can break that work apart from the rest. The system that supports your like thing is your thin Vertical Slice of work. Where the system behind the scenes includes your other layers.

Putting the Ideas Together

Combined, these ideas are Vertical Slicing of work. In Agile, this helps lead to a key concept. Which is incremental delivery. This is very important in agile.

Incremental delivery is about consistent, progressive, and piece-meal progress. Progress on work items and goals. By consistency, you are delivering work at regular times. You also delivery quality at regular times. By progressive, you are building onto prior work items. By piece-meal, I mean that the work is small and you can manage it.

Chapter Four

Benefits from Vertical Slicing

Let us explore some of the benefits gained from Vertical Slicing of user stories.

Getting value sooner

One of the best benefits is gaining value sooner. By breaking work into pieces, those pieces can deliver value on their own. Work is not as tied to all the other pieces of work as it is purposefully broken into stand alone work items.

This allows you to put pieces of work into place sooner. Pieces that you can go and execute on in short order. Which, because the work is organized into smaller pieces, you can also organize around the most important work items. So now only to you get to see value quickly, you can get the highest value items without waiting on other work items that can be done separately and later.

Easier to prioritize work

You can weigh pieces of work against others more easily. In other words, its easier to compare work and see which ones to do. When you prioritize the work, it stands to reason that the higher priority items will deliver higher value. Not always the case, but often so.

By having work items organized into smaller vertical slices of work, you can start to understand relative value amongst all the work better. Which allows better decisions on what work items to go and do next.

Value gain over time

Consistent delivery allows you to build value over time. Pieces of work stack on each other. They accumulate value. Each piece on its own delivers value. However, over time, the value is greater as you complete more pieces.

This is really an important concept, yet sometimes it gets lost in the weeds. We all want things now. The sooner the better. But, if you, your team, your stakeholders, etc, all can get on the same page and start to execute on a piece of work, then move onto the next thing. You are creating an environment where you will consistently deliver value. You will deliver that value over a longer period of time. The deliver, the pace, and the work effort are more sustainable.

Building understanding

Another benefit is that it becomes easier to understand the value of backlog work. You can more easily see the value in the backlog. Because you have broken apart the work into more pieces. Which, allows you to assign work its own value. Which enables easier ranking against other work. The lines between work become more distinct. This helps greatly with priorities.

Consistent Feedback

Consistent and frequent feedback is so important. You need honest and critical feedback. The team uses it to learn and adjust. Doing Vertical Slicing in Agile, you help enable a better feedback loop.

Feedback is one of the most important building blocks in Agile software development. When you can get good feedback, and do so consistently and frequently, you will build the right things and deliver tremendous value. Smaller pieces of work, via Vertical Slices, allows that feedback.

Avoid working on things of low or no value

By working in smaller pieces, you enable more frequent course corrections. If working on something that is low or no value, once you have a portion of this ready enough, you will get feedback for the team and determine the question on value. Because of the smaller pieces of work, you can then shift to other more valuable work.

The alternative to this is when the team works on large chunks of work, with large timeframes involved. There is often little to no user feedback during the development. Thus, you can do a lot of work, only to find it needs to be fixed or course corrected on. When working in smaller pieces, even in the worst case scenario, the wasted effort is mitigated.

Enables response to changing business priorities

Often business priorities can change. Where you thought you would work on something, but you have to change direction and work on other things. By working in smaller pieces of work, this change is enabled. Because changing priorities are often directed by potential value gained for the organization, being able to shift focus only helps the company to gain value

Allows just enough work to meet goals

A great thing about this way of working, that is much related to above comments on working on items of value, is that you can complete just enough work on something to get the value you need. Then because you work in incremental portions, once the gain needed is there, you can set that down and move on to the next priority item. If working on large portions of work or work that is not stand alone in functionality, you would not be able to do this.

Chapter Five

Agile and Waterfall Time to Delivery

Vertical Slicing the work enables incremental and consistent delivery of value in Agile software development.

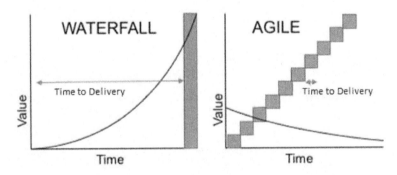

Agile Time to Delivery

I have included this diagram showing how the Vertical Slice helps delivery. The diagram shows the agile sprint flow. You gain value when the work is done. If you compare to the Waterfall flow, it takes much longer before done. Thus, Agile gains value more quickly. Additionally, at each stage, you have the ability to learn and adjust course.

As opposed to Waterfall, where the time frame is longer. There is much less ability to course correct. The pieces of work is a big part of the Agile flow. As smaller pieces of work enable shorter sprints. They also enable the build, learn and adjust concept. Where the team can learn and do things better.

Contrasting with Vertical Slices, you have Horizontal Slices of the System. Horizontal Slicing of work is the end-to-end piece of work.

This is to say it is a piece of work across one system layer. By this, it could be the entire user interface or the entire database. The drawbacks of this route can be severe. As you create functionality without knowing the rest of the system. It's difficult to create a new database accurately. Especially without knowing the front end fields it supports.

Vertical Slicing Gains Business Value

You might also know Vertical Slices as Value Slices. Meaning that it is a piece of work, that delivers value. It is important to remember the connection to delivering value. Above all, Agile and Vertical Slicing user stories is about providing value and doing so step by step. It is all part of incremental delivery to the stakeholder and users. Gain value faster when you boost your delivery.

Incremental delivery allows for quick timelines. In other words, work is done in short sprints. Incremental delivery opens the door to good feedback loops. As a result, it helps with quick learning by the agile team. Lastly, incremental delivery allows for changes along the way. It is flexible and responsive to changing needs. Responding to change helps the team to build the right things.

This helps avoid the pitfalls of Waterfall development. Where you can be too far along to effectively respond to change. The quick feedback loop in agile helps that. It allows for course correction. Which you get from Vertical Slices of work.

Chapter Six

5 Best Questions to Break Up User Stories Into Vertical Slices

The below questions are a great guide to help with these ideas. These questions will help break up your user stories into Vertical Slices of work. User stories that you can deliver on and gain value on immediately. Splitting your user stories like this is a great Agile practice. Using these questions will get you moving forward on it in no time.

These ideas are how you can write better user stories. More importantly though, user stories that are likely to be completed. Use them to help break up your deliverables. Making the work more manageable and enabling completion.

1. Is there a core set of functions? Which are most important or most of what is needed. If not a core function or not important, it can be moved to the product backlog for later consideration.
2. Are there business rules or logic? Can you do these separately?
3. Is there a workflow? Within the workflow are there stops, where you can divide before/after the stop? Or, if multiple branches of a workflow, could you do a happy path through first? Then add more variations to it with additional work.
4. Do you receive, manage, or update date from multiple processes or interfaces? Split based on those variations.
5. Is there speed, performance, timing, or quality involved? Can you first get something to function, and later add the additional metrics for these?

Chapter 7

Last Thoughts on Vertical Slicing of Work

Vertical Slicing is an important concept in Agile methodologies. It helps the team with many practices. If not using it, you should consider using it in your software projects now! Back to the cherry on top. The last piece of the cake is that cherry on top and it is the value delivered by using this process.

You will find you can boost your delivery and enable quality software completion. To reiterate its benefits, it will help with the below:

- incremental delivery
- gaining business value
- consistent feedback loops
- responding to change
- builds team understanding

Closing

Contact and upcoming content

As always, I like to continue learning and further my ideas. Drop me a line if you would like to discuss further.

Find more @ Agile Rant

TJ Rerob is a founder and top contributor at Agile Rant. Agile Rant is an online publication on Agile, software development, product, teamwork, leadership and other modern practices. Blog postings explore questions and issues and dive into items to help explore and find answers.

https://www.agilerant.info

Please sign up for the Agile Rant newsletter

@ https://www.agilerant.info/connect-with-agile-rant/.
There you will gain access to deals on books, notices on upcoming content, access to the existing library of content, and more. Your email will never be sold or spammed. This is for readers interested in more Agile Rant content.

Lastly, feel free to connect via our social media accounts:

https://www.instagram.com/agile_rant
https://www.twitter.com/AgileRant
https://www.facebook.com/Agile.Rant1.0/

Upcoming ebook

The Beautiful Art of Not Doing Work

Always aiming to provide good info and earning your business

In my ebooks I always aim to provide useful, but concise information. I want concepts and ideas to be readily available to be taken and put into practice. I don't aim for over the top elaboration, but try to get to the point. We are all busy, and learning new things shouldn't take hours upon hours. Thus my texts are more concise than some other offerings out there.

Regardless, if you don't feel like you come away with good information or what you expected, I would love to hear about it. Improvement is the name of the game, for myself as well.

Additionally, if I can help to get you to a place where you would consider leaving me a positive review, I would greatly enjoy the chance to do so. I have multiple other offerings already published, and others in the works. Please email me at tj_rerob@outlook.com, if I can help to earn a positive review.

Printed in Great Britain
by Amazon

36094561R00020